SCHOLA

GRADE K–1

MW01269212

Success With

Traditional Manuscript

New York • Toronto • London • Auckland • Sydney
Mexico City • New Delhi • Hong Kong • Buenos Aires

Teaching Resources

State Standards Correlations

To find out how this book helps you meet your state's standards, log on to **www.scholastic.com/ssw**

Written by Jill Kaufman
Cover design by Ka-Yeon Kim-Li
Interior illustrations by Carol Tiernon
Interior design by Quack & Company

ISBN-13 978-0-545-20073-8
ISBN-10 0-545-20073-3

6 7 8 9 10 40 17 16 15 14

Introduction

Parents and teachers alike will find this book to be a valuable teaching tool. Children will enjoy the humorous art as they learn and practice traditional handwriting. All 26 letters of the alphabet will be mastered through practice writing letters, words, and sentences. Step-by-step letter formation, writing upper- and lowercase letters, and writing numbers, days of the week, and months are just some of the activities included. Teaching these valuable handwriting skills to eager young learners will be a rewarding experience. Remember to praise the children for their efforts and successes!

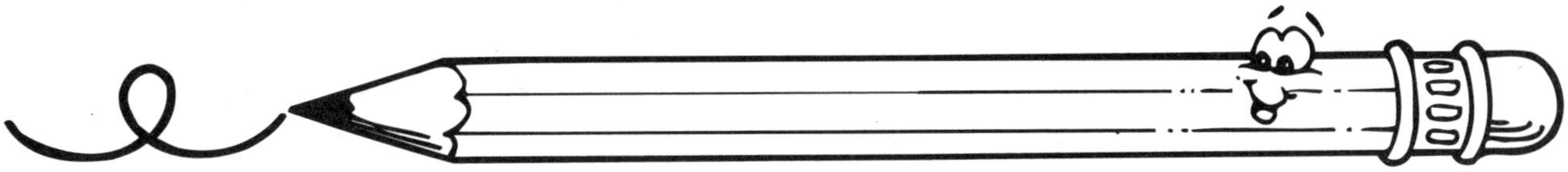

Table of Contents

Name ______________________________

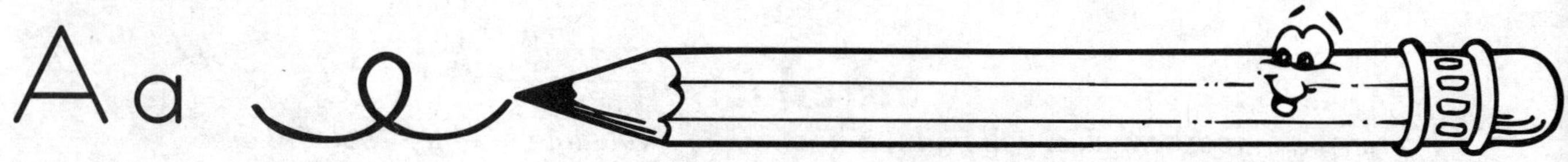

Trace and write.

A A A

a a a a

A a

Adam Ape is active.

Annie asked Alice.

Name ______________________________

Bb

Trace and write.

B B B

b b b b

B b

Betsy bee buzzes.

Bobby buys balloons.

Name ______________________

Cc

Trace and write.

C C C

c c c c

Cc

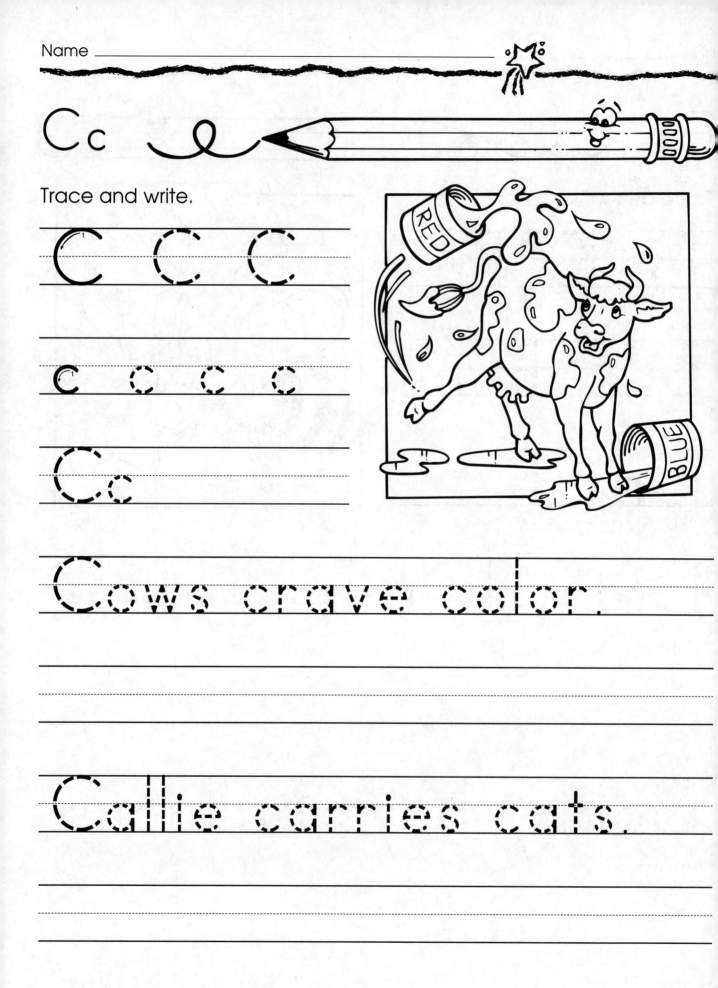

Cows crave color.

Callie carries cats.

Name ______________________________

D d

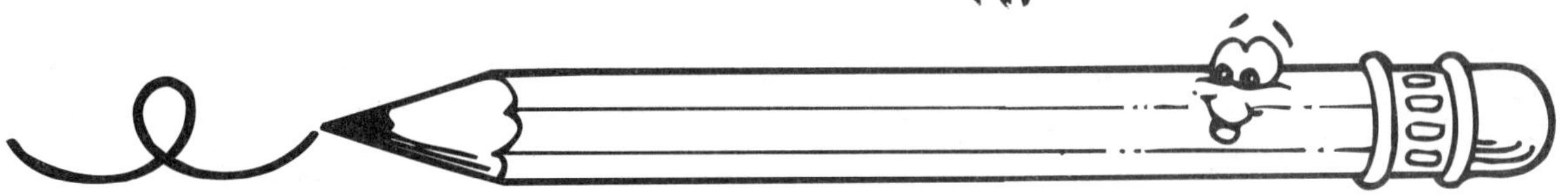

Trace and write.

D D D D

d d d d

D d

Dandy Duck dances.

Dragons draw dogs.

Name ______________________________

E e

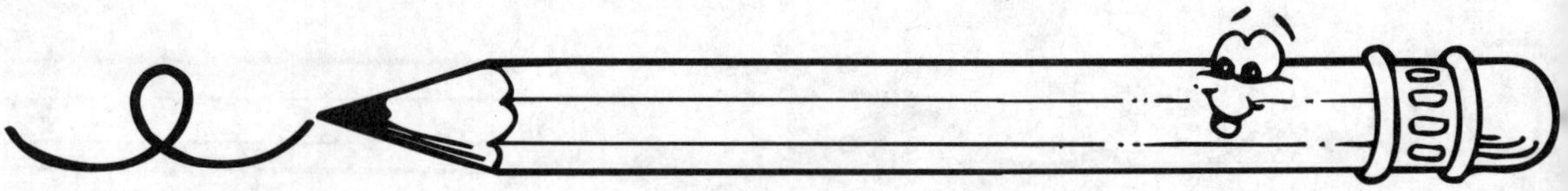

Trace and write.

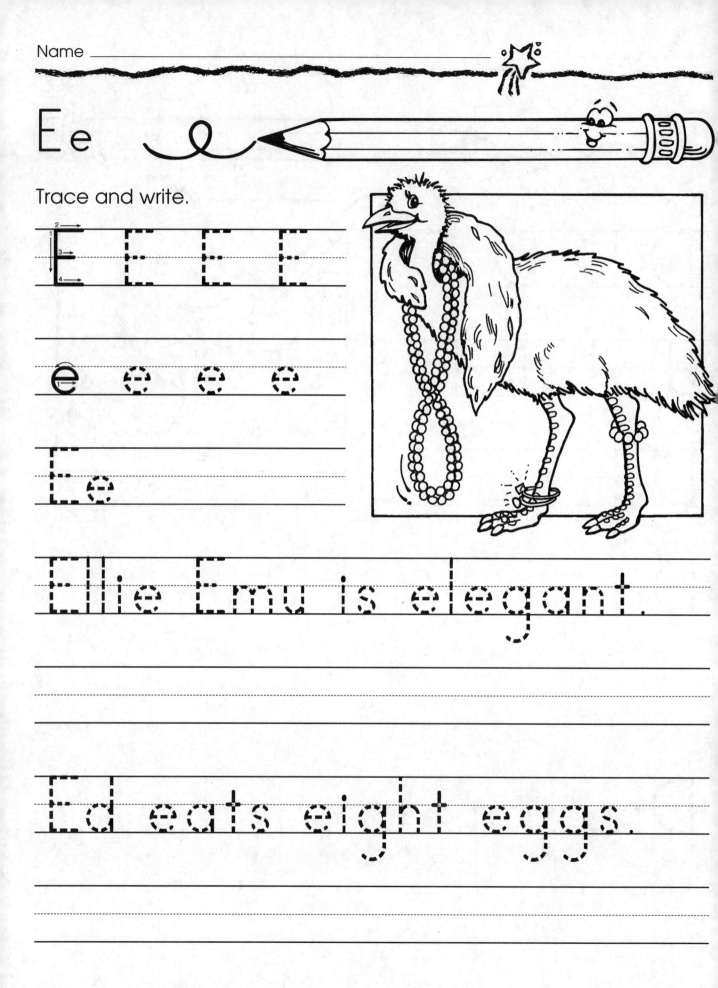

E E E E

e e e e

E e

Ellie Emu is elegant.

Ed eats eight eggs.

Name ______________________________

F f

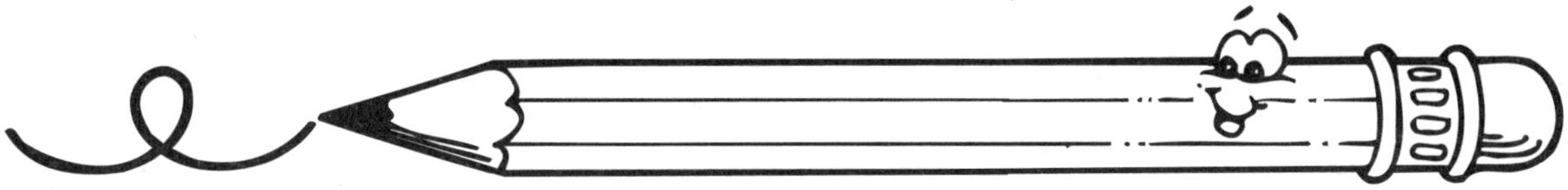

Trace and write.

F F F

f f f f

F f

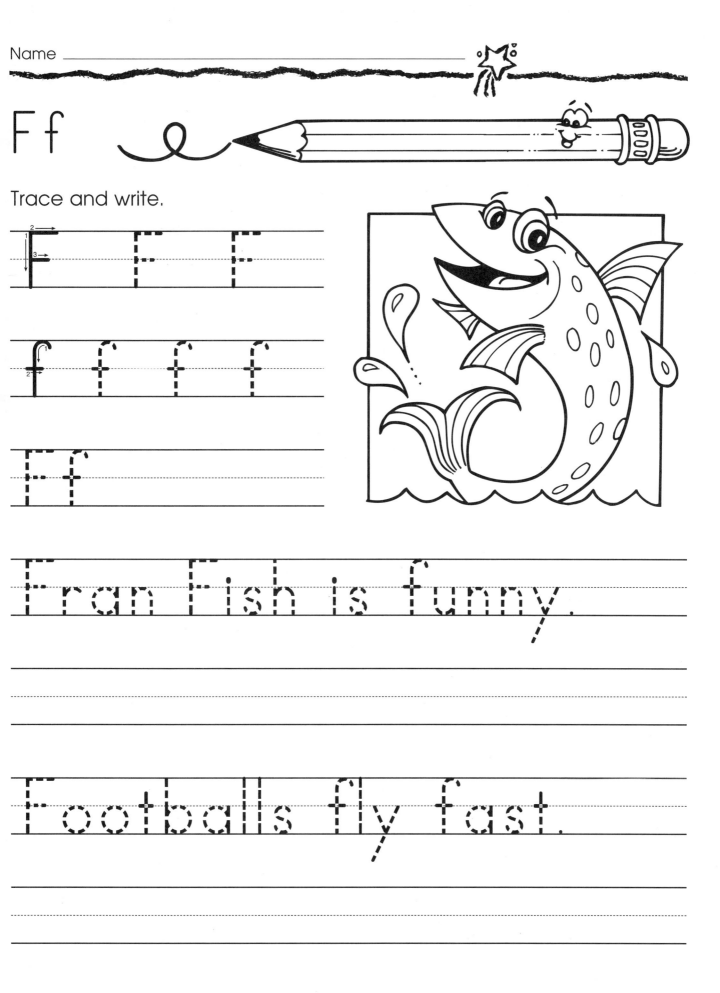

Fran Fish is funny.

Footballs fly fast.

Name

Gg

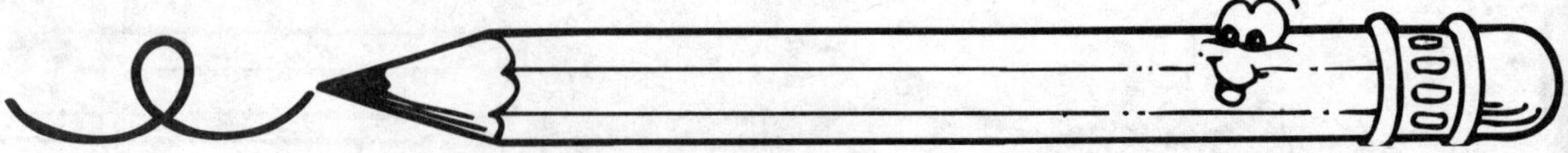

Trace and write.

G G G

g g g g

Gg

Gus Goose giggles.

Greta grows greens.

Name ______________________________

Hh

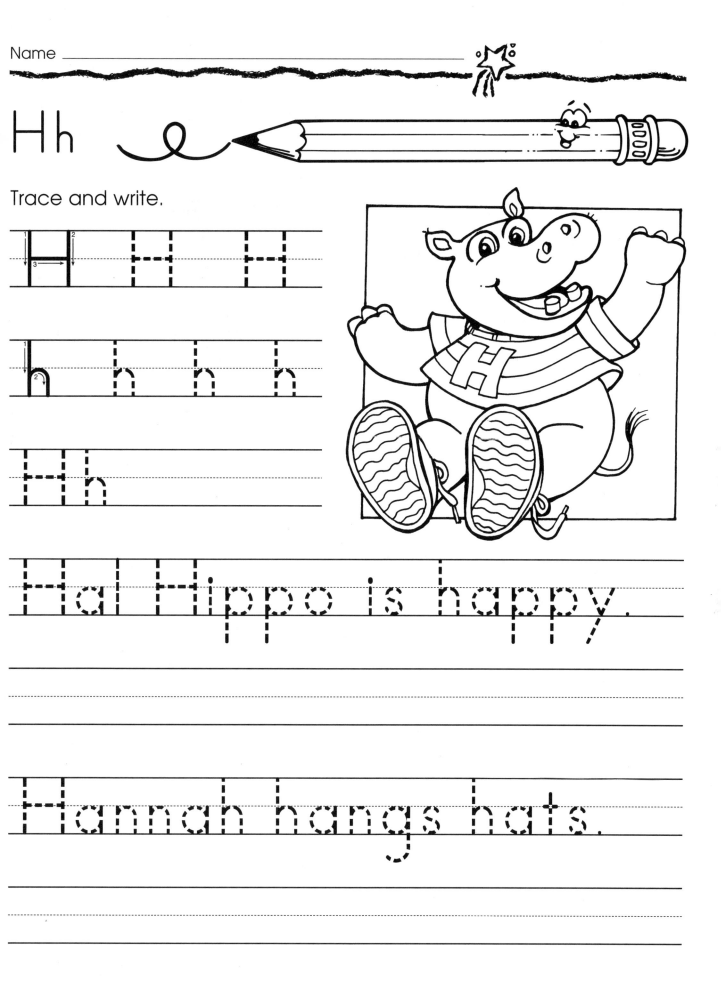

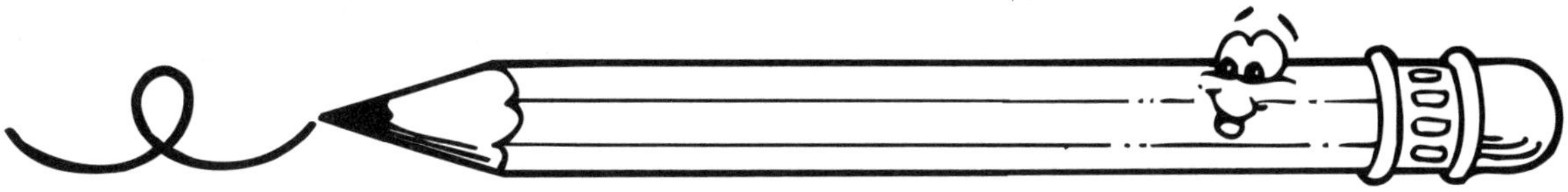

Trace and write.

H H H

h h h h

H h

Hal Hippo is happy.

Hannah hangs hats.

Name ______________________________

I i

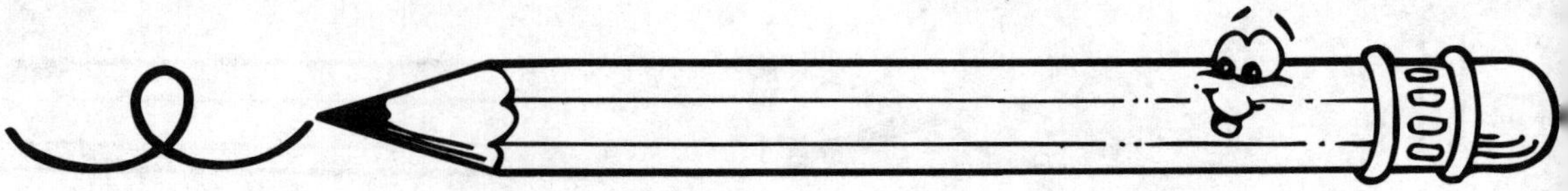

Trace and write.

I I I I

i i i i

I i

Irina Iguana is itchy.

Invite Irving inside.

Name ______________________________

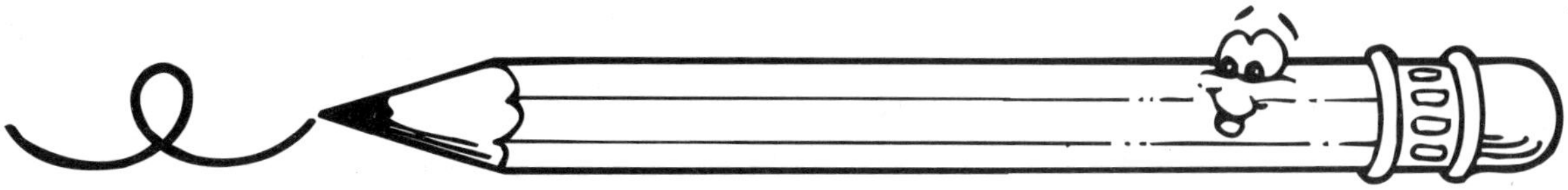

J j

Trace and write.

J J J

j j j j

J j

Jim Jellyfish is jazzy.

Jill juggles jelly jars.

Name ______________________________

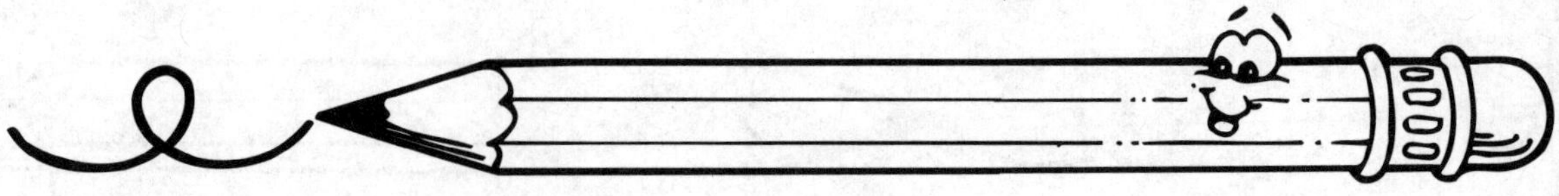

K k

Trace and write.

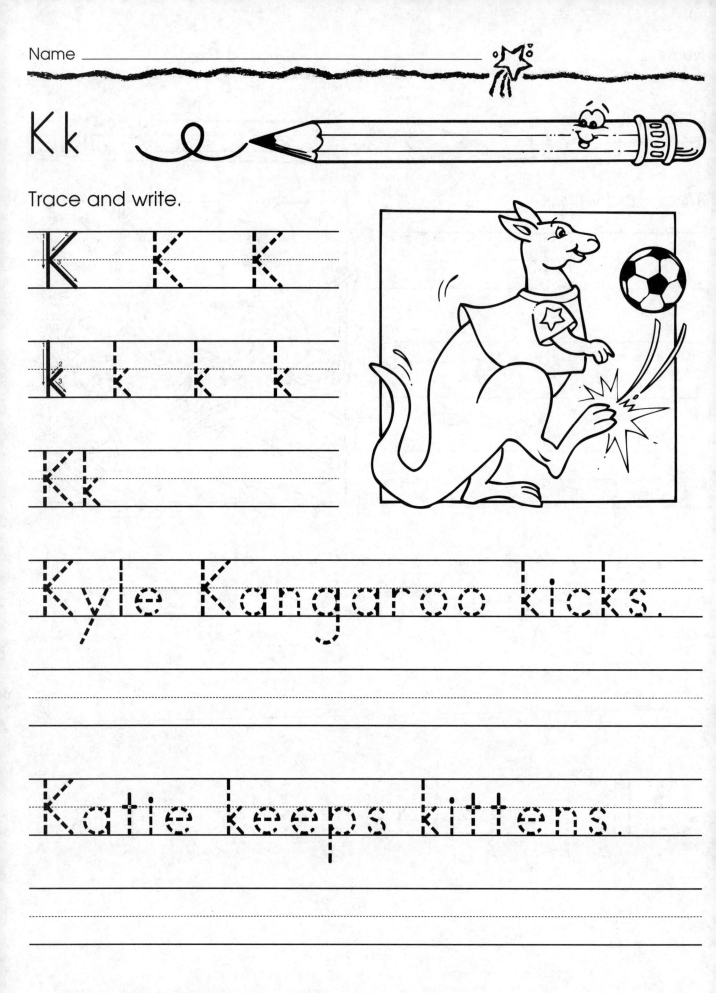

K K K

k k k k

K k

Kyle Kangaroo kicks.

Katie keeps kittens.

Name

Ll

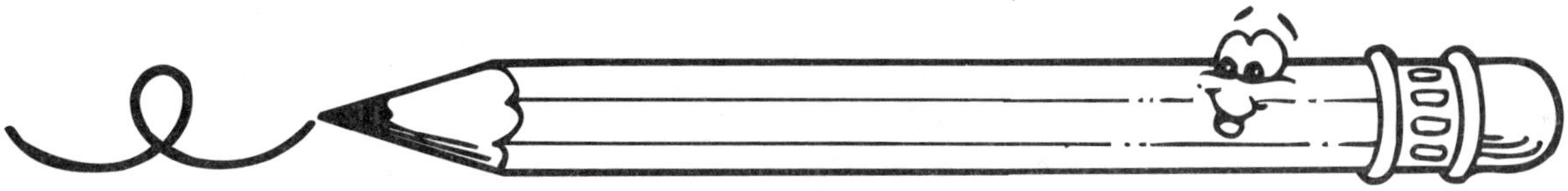

Trace and write.

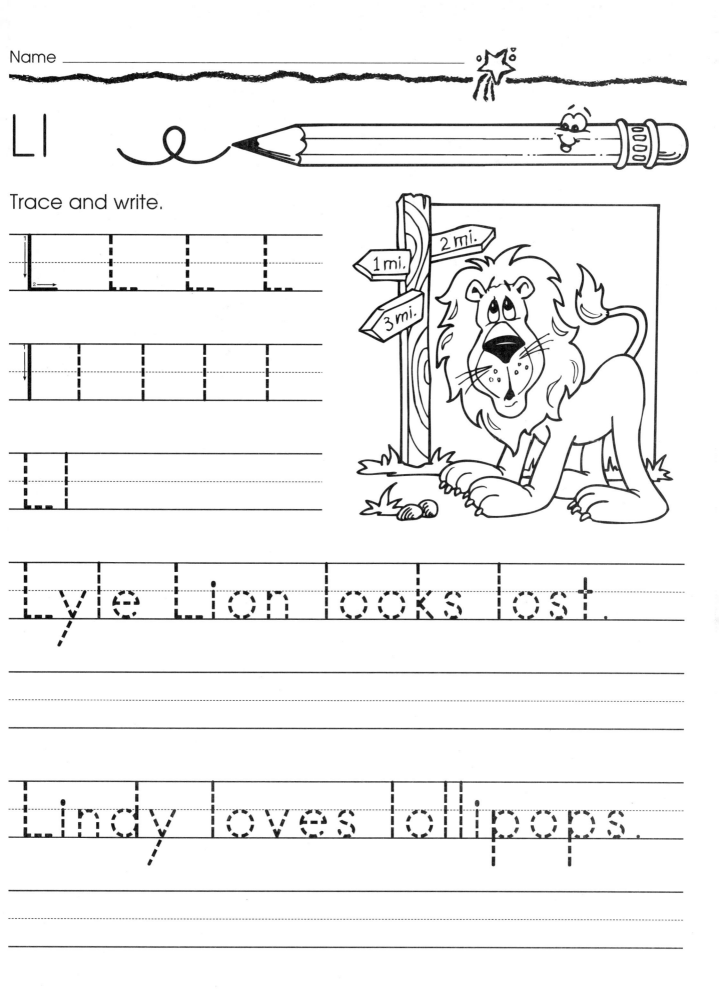

Lyle Lion looks lost.

Lindy loves lollipops.

Name ______________________________

Mm

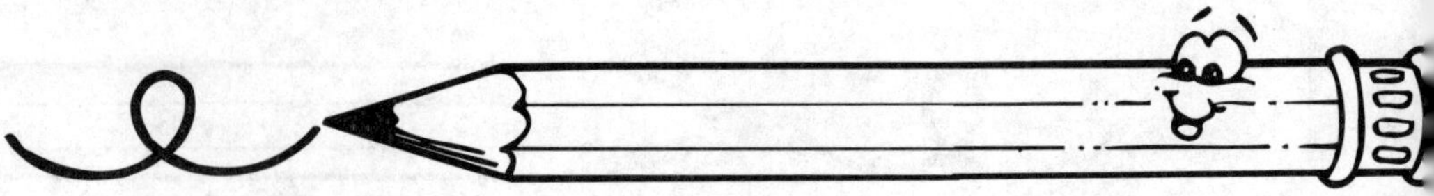

Trace and write.

M M M

m m m

Mm

Mike Mouse is messy.

Mom met Madeline.

Name ____

Nn

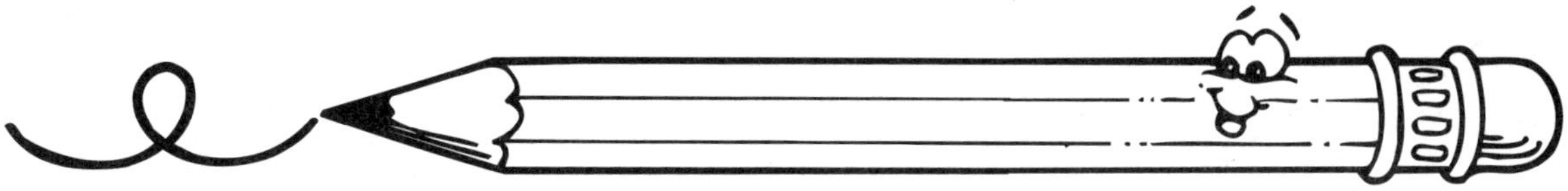

Trace and write.

N N N

n n n n

N n

Nikki Newt needs naps.

Nurse Ned nibbles.

Name

Oo

Trace and write.

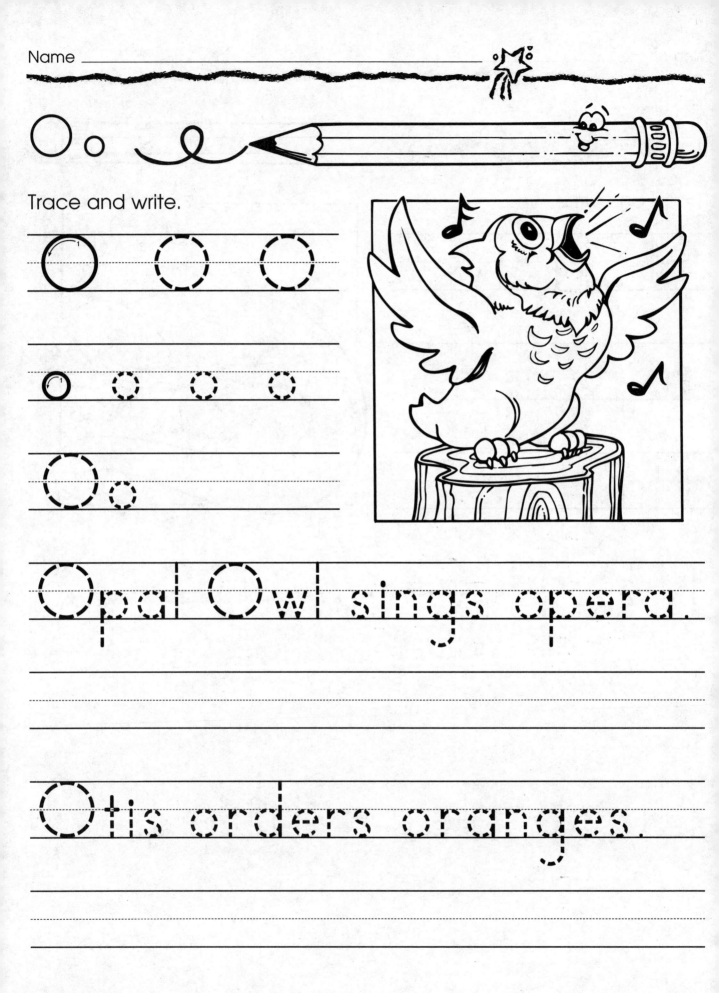

O O O

o o o o

O o

Opal Owl sings opera.

Otis orders oranges.

Name

Pp

Trace and write.

P P P

p p p p

P p

Pam Pig paid a penny.

Peter Pig says please.

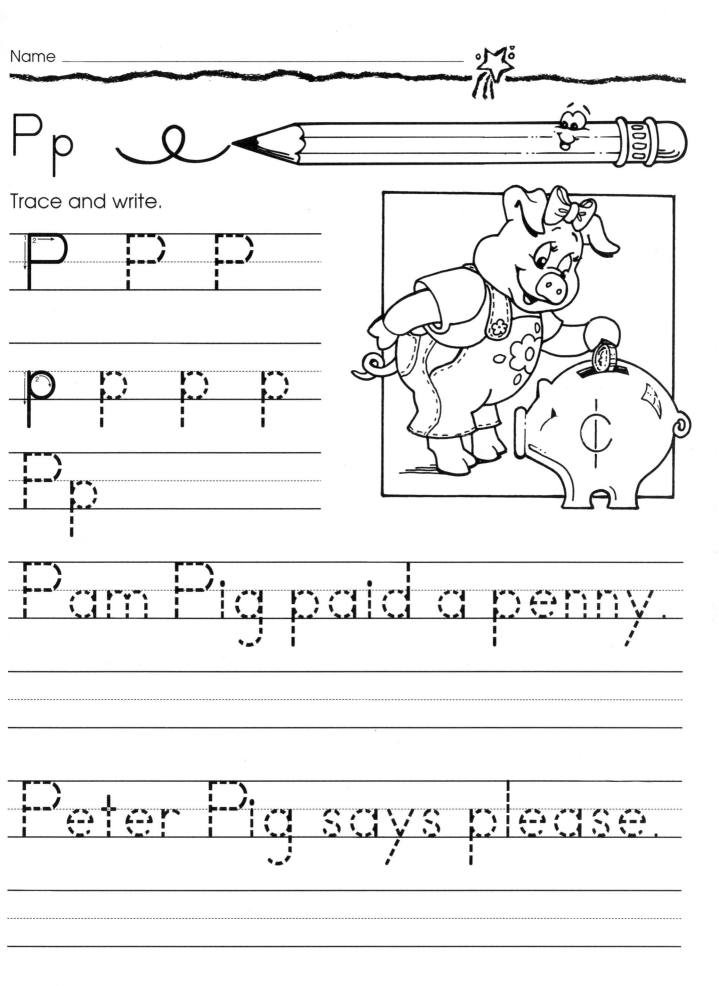

Name ______________________________

Q q

Trace and write.

Q Q Q

q q q q

Q q

Quinn Quail is quiet.

Quebec is quite nice.

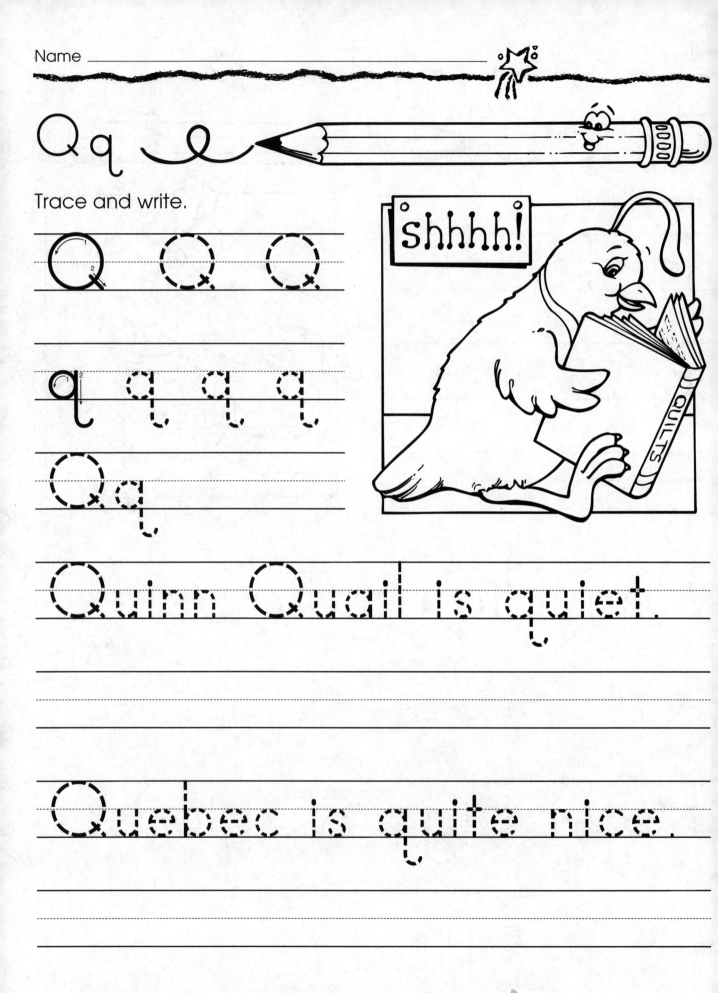

Name ______________________________

Rr

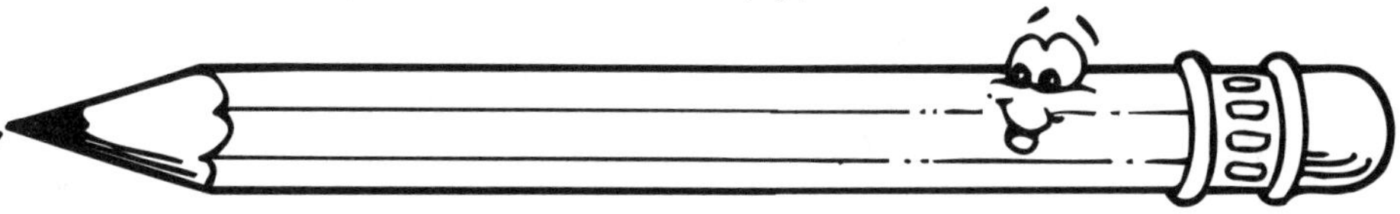

Trace and write.

R R R

r r r r

Rr

Randy Rabbit races.

Robin reads rapidly.

Name ______________________________

Ss

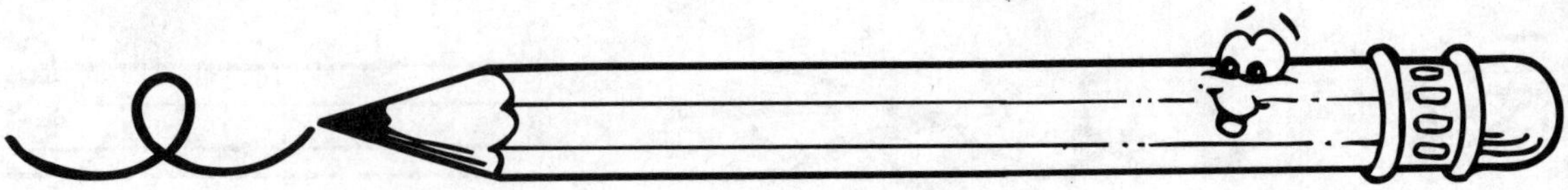

Trace and write.

S S S S

s s s s

S s

Susanna Seal stars.

Sam sees sailboats.

Name ______________________________

Tt

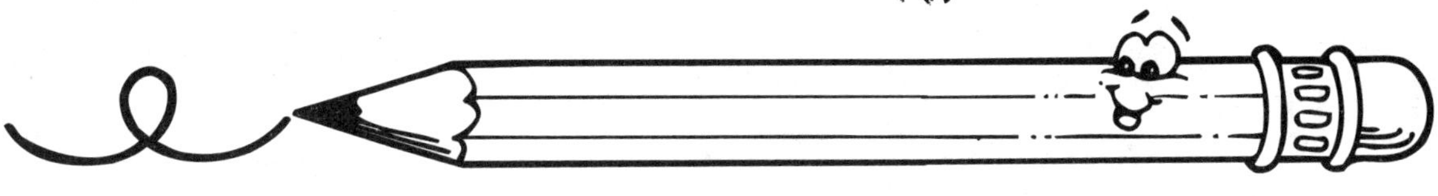

Trace and write.

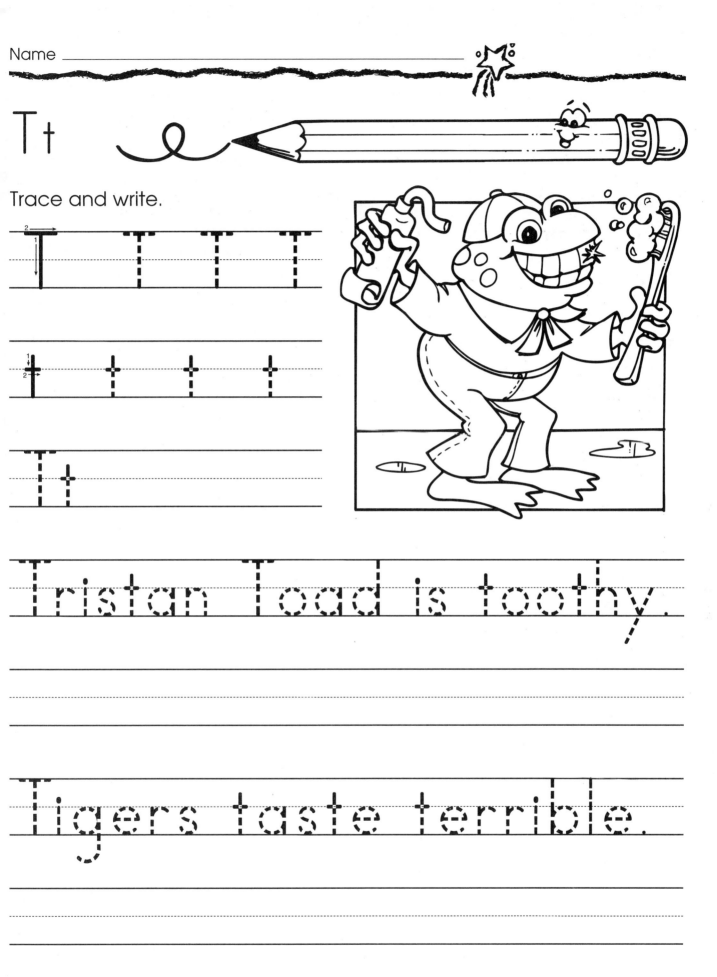

T T T T

t t t t

T t

Tristan Toad is toothy.

Tigers taste terrible.

Name

U u

Trace and write.

U U U U

u u u u

U u

Ula uses an umbrella.

Uncle Uno umpires.

Name ______________________________

Vv

Trace and write.

V V V

v v v v

V v

Vic Vulture is vain.

Vegetables vary.

Name ____________________

Ww

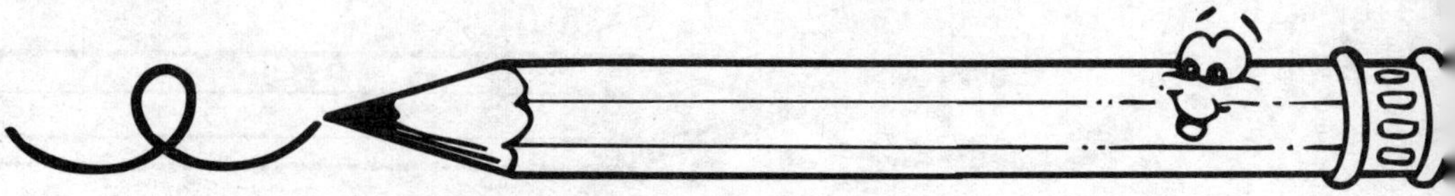

Trace and write.

W W W

w w w w

W w

Will Worm is wealthy.

Wilma wipes windows.

Name ____________________

Xx

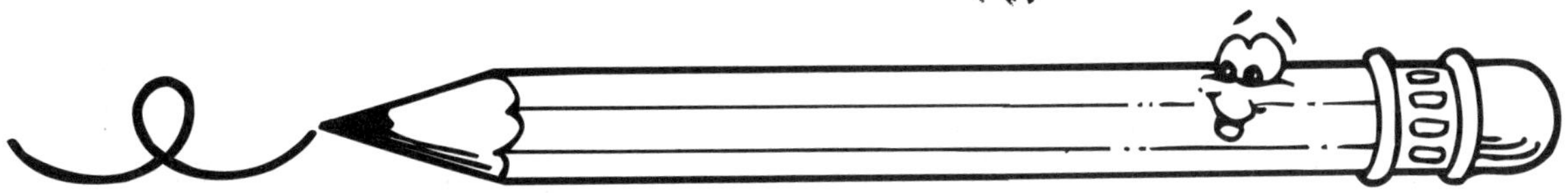

Trace and write.

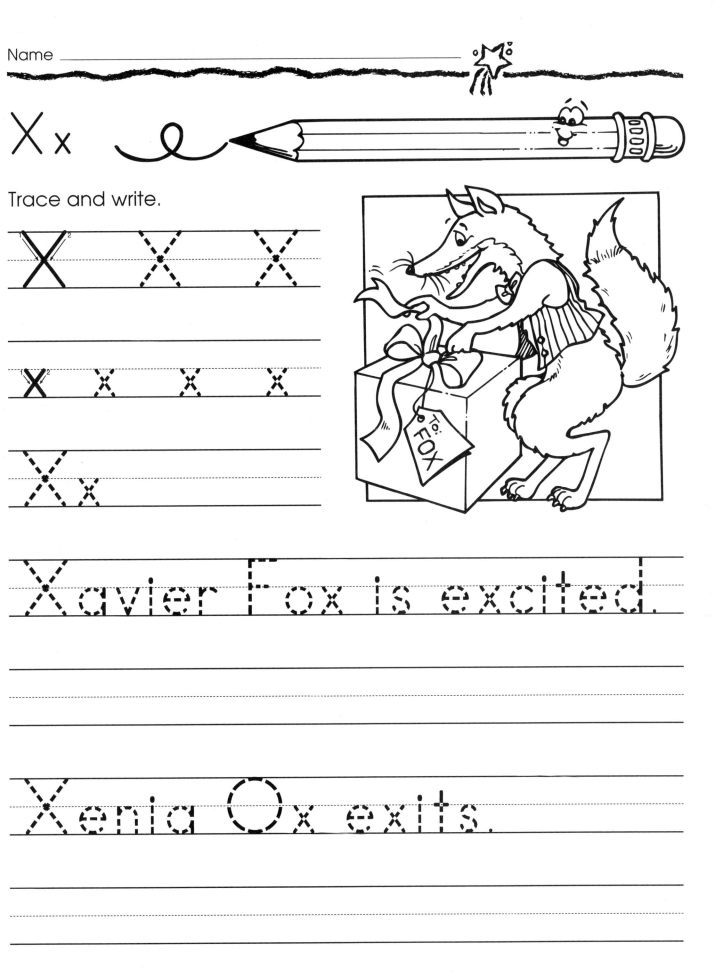

X X X

x x x x

X x

Xavier Fox is excited.

Xenia Ox exits.

Name

Yy

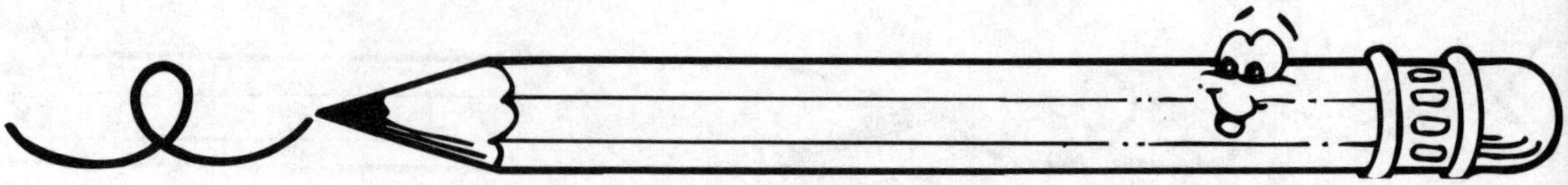

Trace and write.

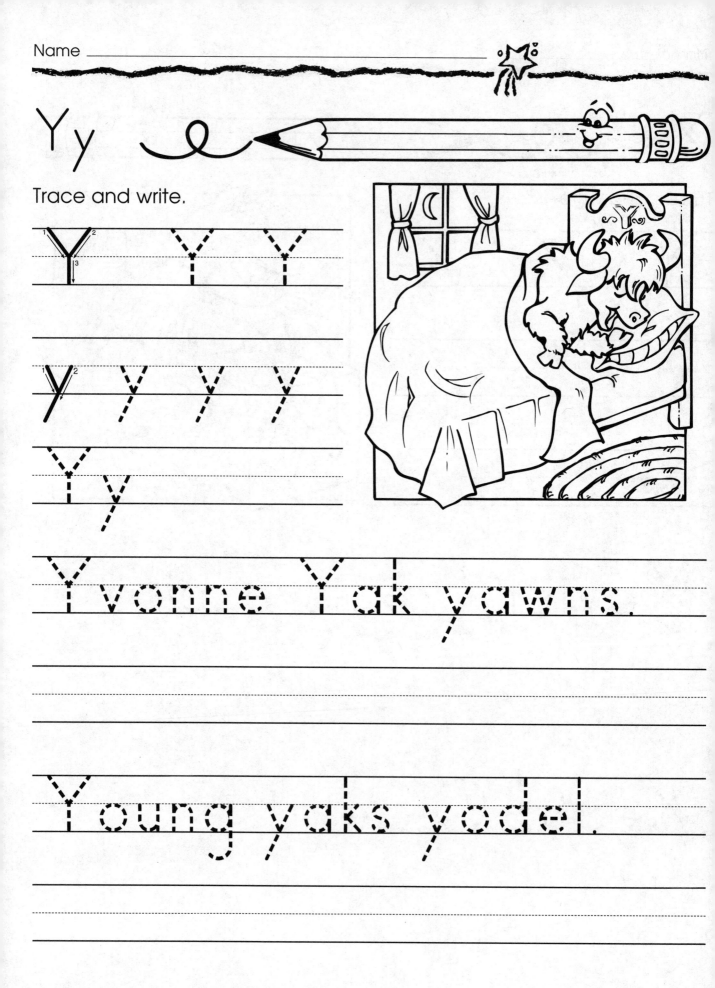

Y Y Y

y y y y

Y y

Yvonne Yak yawns.

Young yaks yodel.

Name ______________________________

Z z

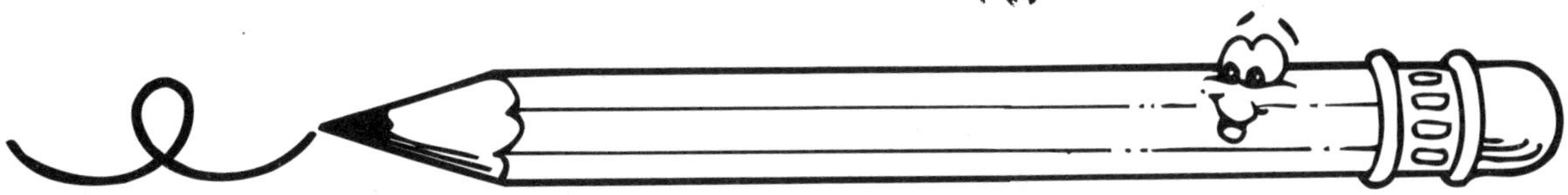

Trace and write.

Z Z Z

z z z z

Z z

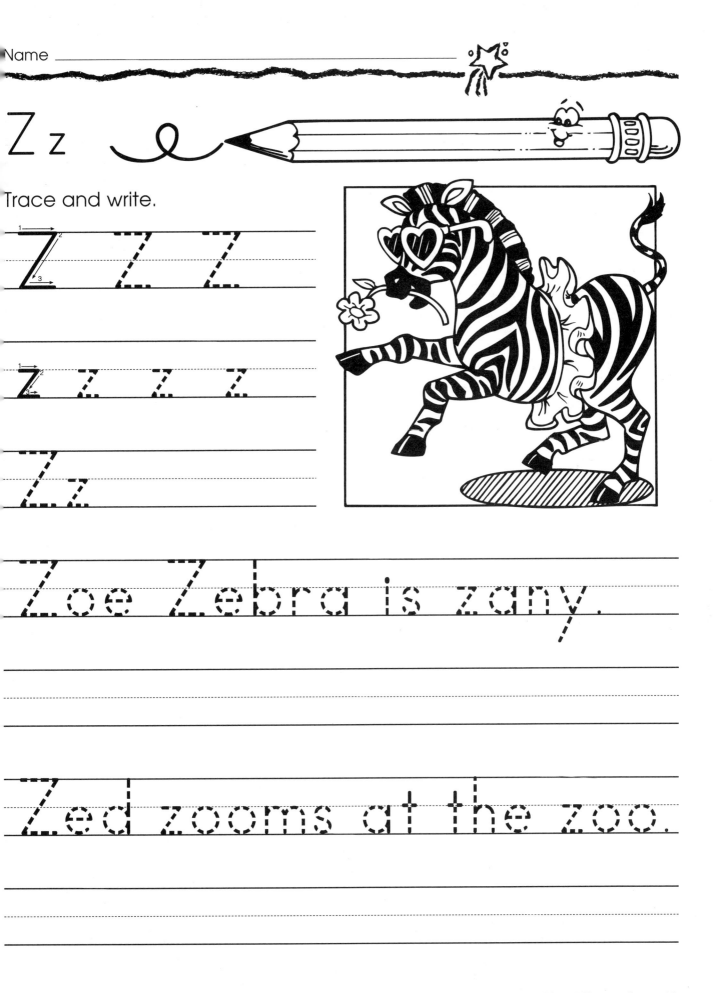

Zoe Zebra is zany.

Zed zooms at the zoo.

Name ____

A–Z

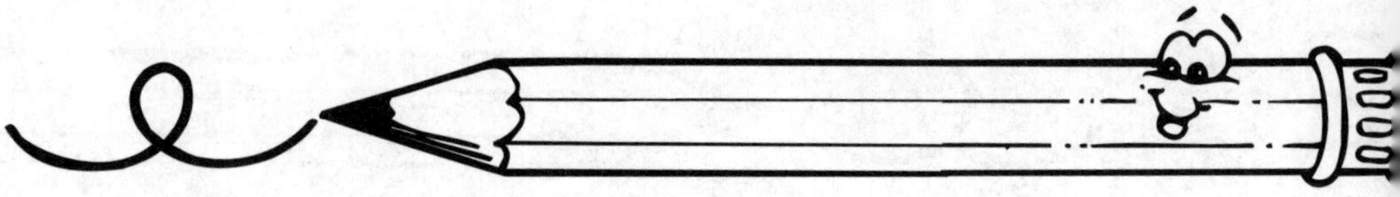

Trace and write.

A B C D E F G H I

J K L M N O P Q

R S T U V W X Y Z

Name ______________________________

a–z

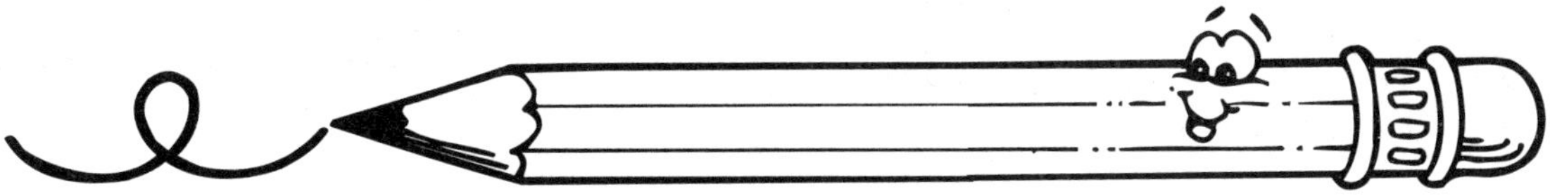

Trace and write.

a b c d e

f g h i j k

l m n o p

q r s t u

v w x y z

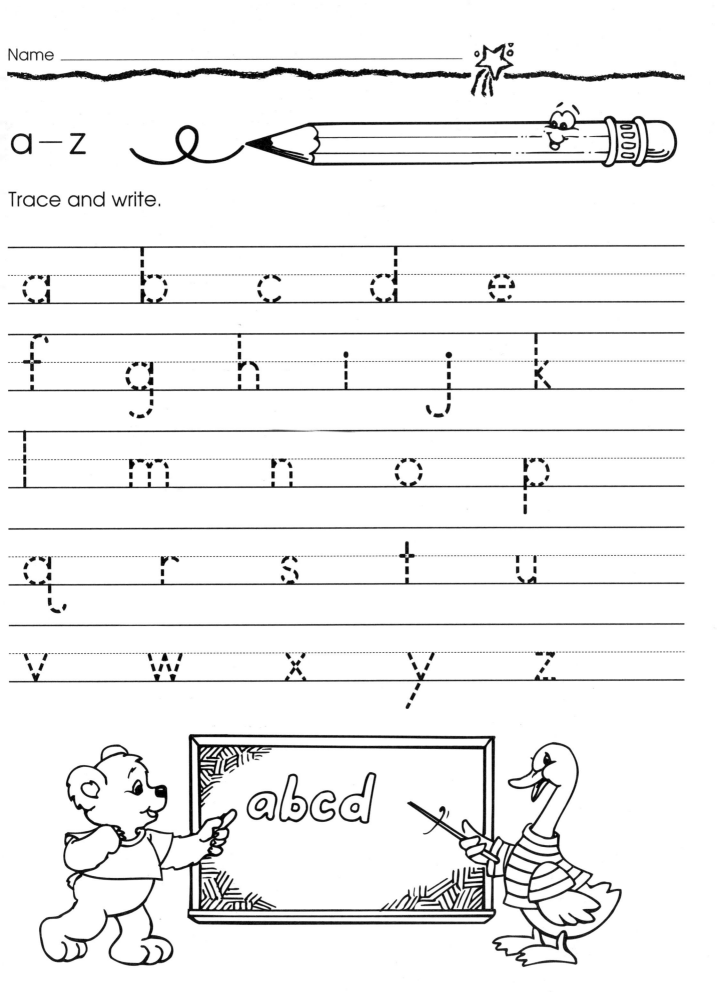

Name ____________________

1–5

Trace and write.

1 1

2 2

3 3

4 4

5 5

Name ______________________________

6–10

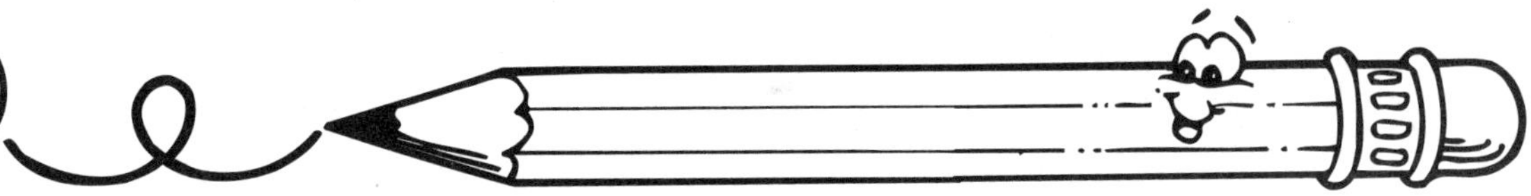

Trace and write.

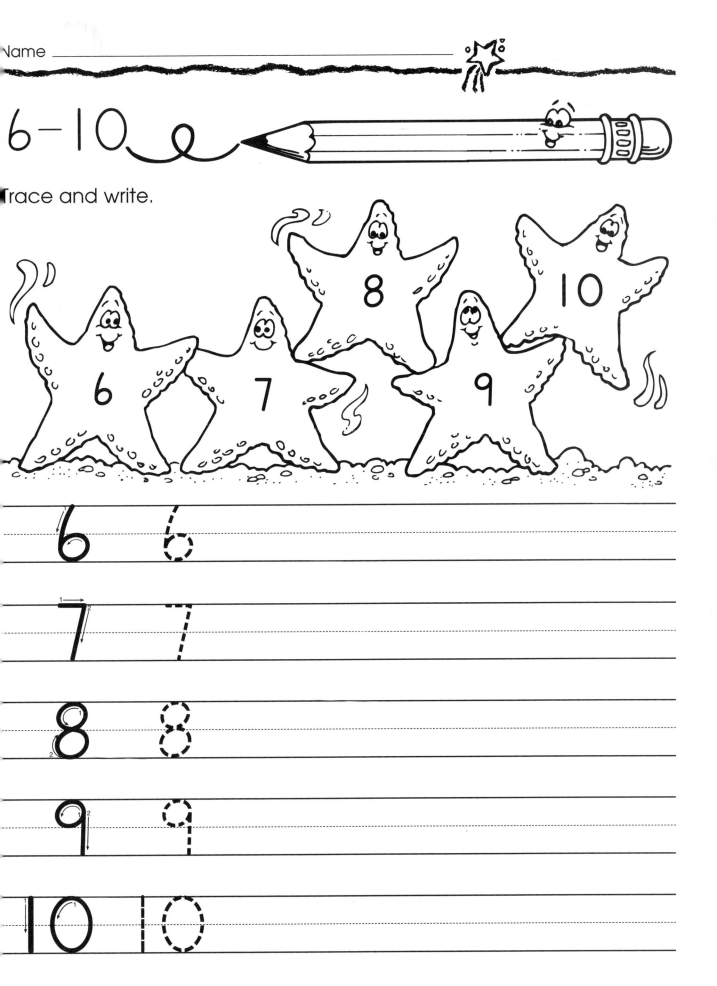

6 6

7 7

8 8

9 9

10 10

Name ______________________________

Color Words

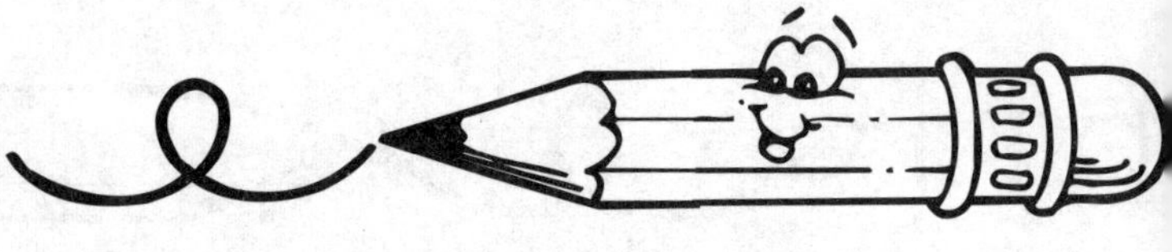

Trace and write.

red

yellow

blue

green

orange

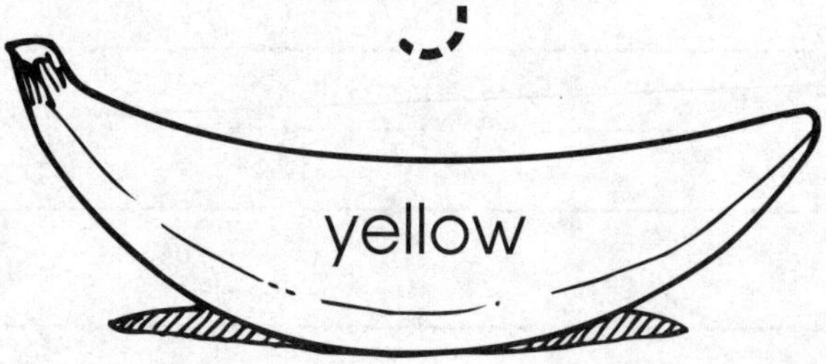

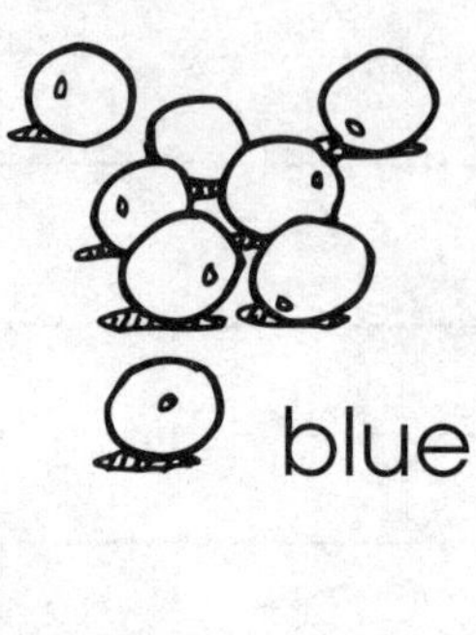

Name ______________________________

More Color Words

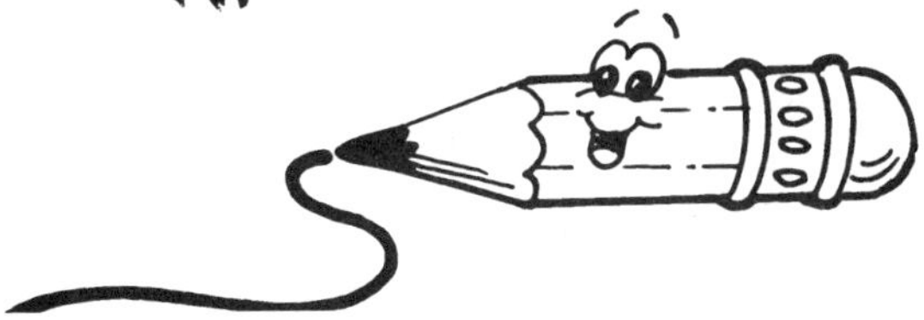

Trace and write.

purple

brown

black

white

pink

Name ______________________________

Number Words

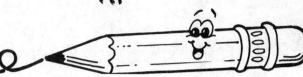

Trace and write.

1 one

2 two

3 three

4 four

5 five

Name ________________________________

More Number Words

Trace and write.

6 six

7 seven

8 eight

9 nine

10 ten

Name ______________________________

Shapes

Trace and write.

oval

heart

circle

square

triangle

diamond

rectangle

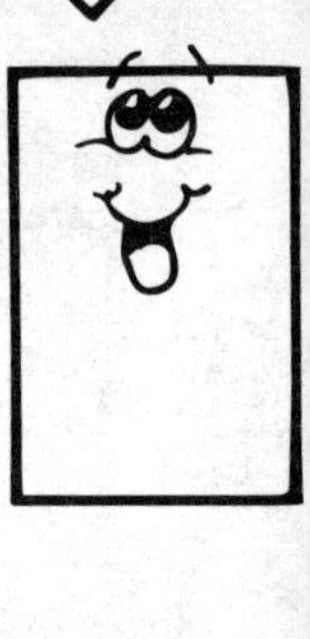

Name ______________________________

Days of the Week

Trace and write.

Sunday

Monday

Tuesday

Wednesday

Thursday

Friday

Saturday

Name ____________________

Months

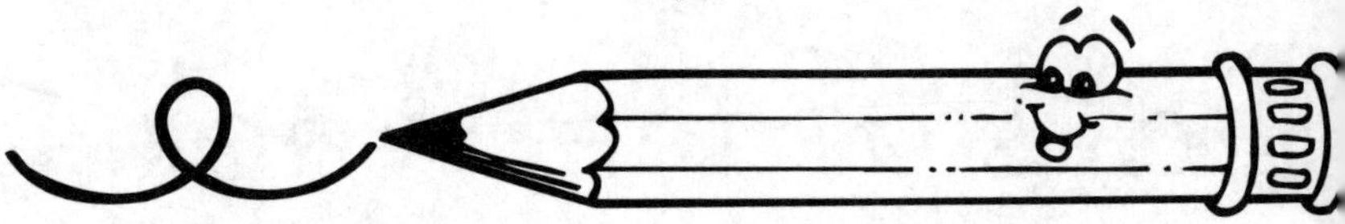

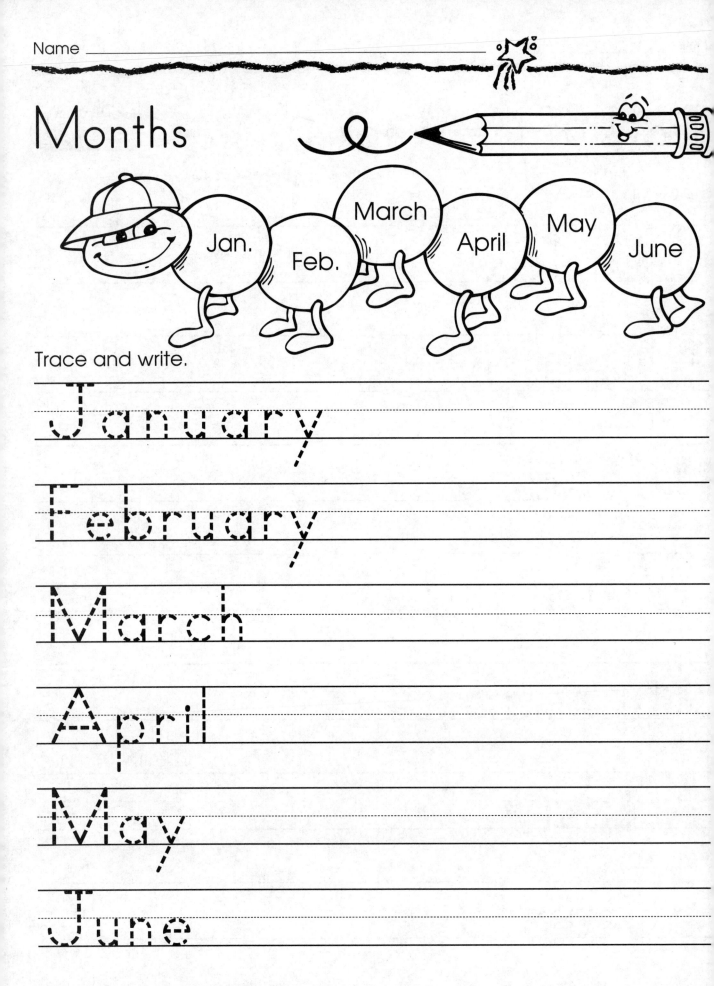

Trace and write.

January

February

March

April

May

June

Name ______________________________

Months

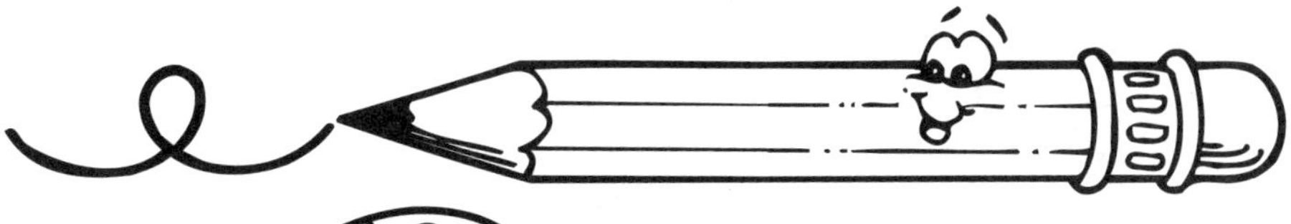

Trace and write.

July

August

September

October

November

December

Name ____________________

Special Days

Write each special day.

New Year's Day

Valentine's Day

Presidents' Day

St. Patrick's Day

Mother's Day

Father's Day

Fourth of July

Name ______________________________

Special Days

Write each special day.

Labor Day

Halloween

Veterans Day

Thanksgiving

Hannukah

Christmas

Kwanzaa

Name ____________________

Animals From A to Z

Write the animal names on the lines below.

alligator
bear
cougar
duck

elk
frog
giraffe
horse

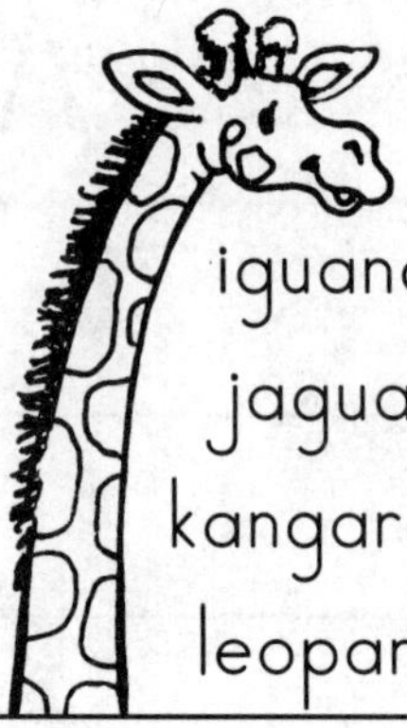

iguana
jaguar
kangaroo
leopard

moose
newt
ostrich

Name ______________________________

Animals From A to Z

Write the animal names on the lines below.

parrot
quail
raccoon

squirrel
tiger
urchin

vulture
whale
X-ray fish

yak
zebra

Name ______________________________

The Continents

Write the names of the continents.

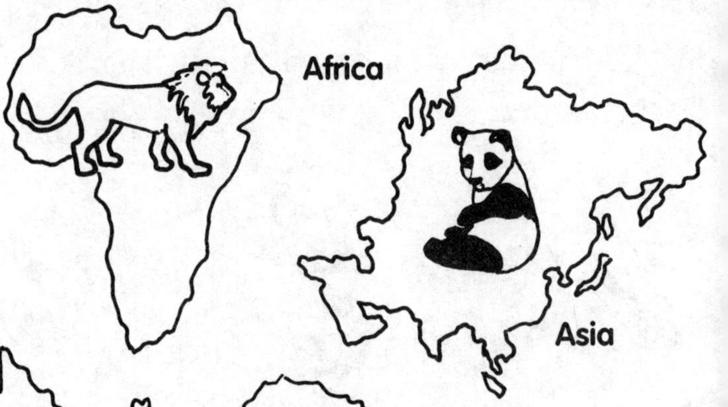

Africa

Asia

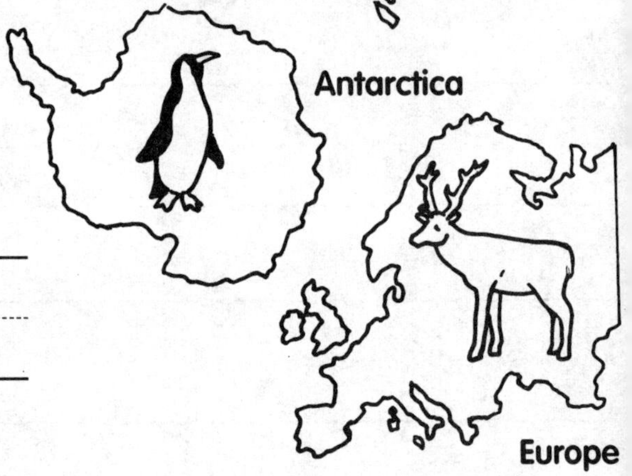

Australia

Antarctica

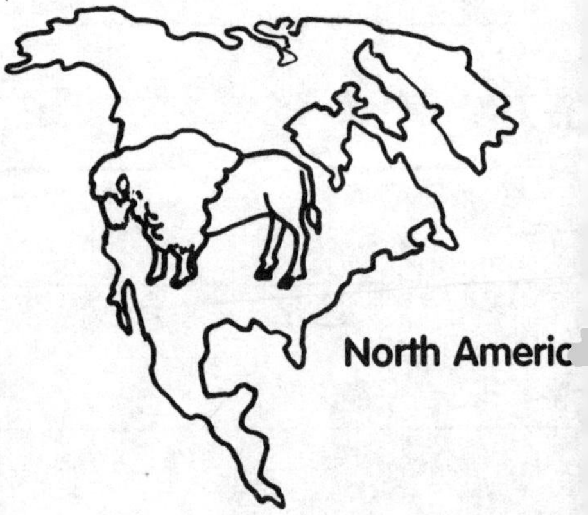

Europe

North America

South America

Name

The Planets

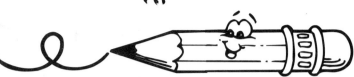

Write the names of the planets.

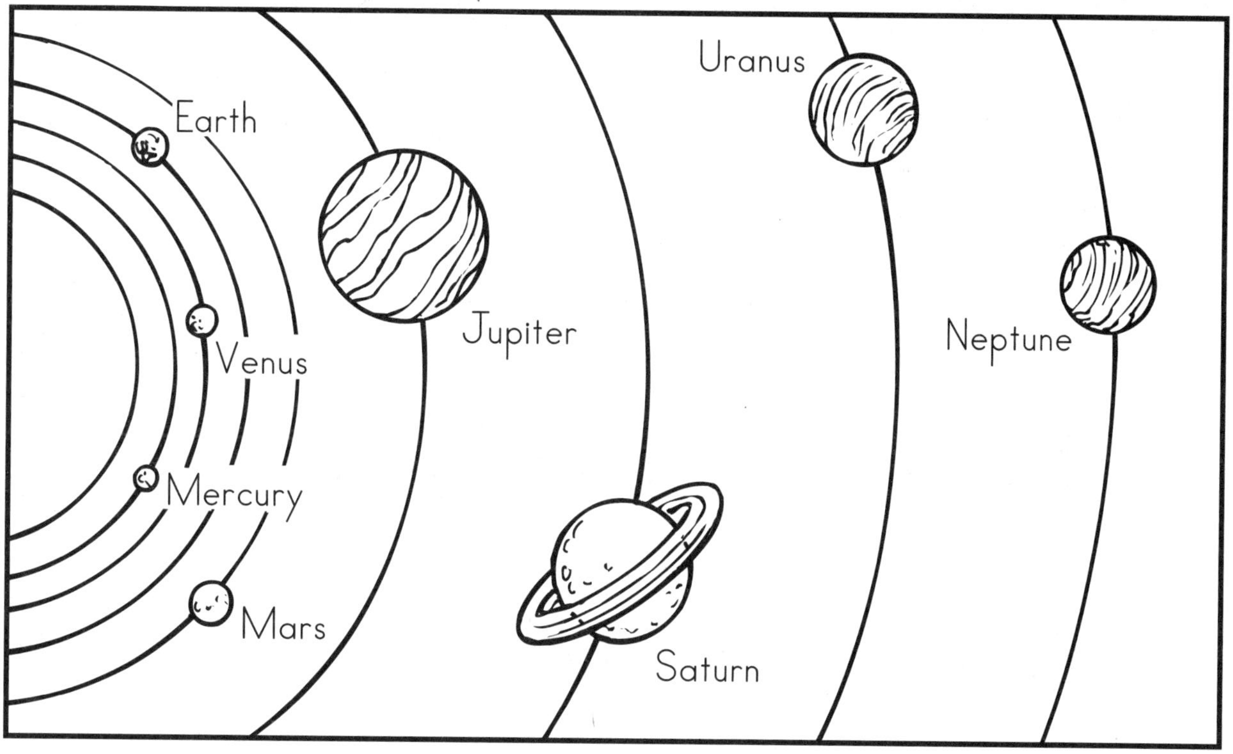

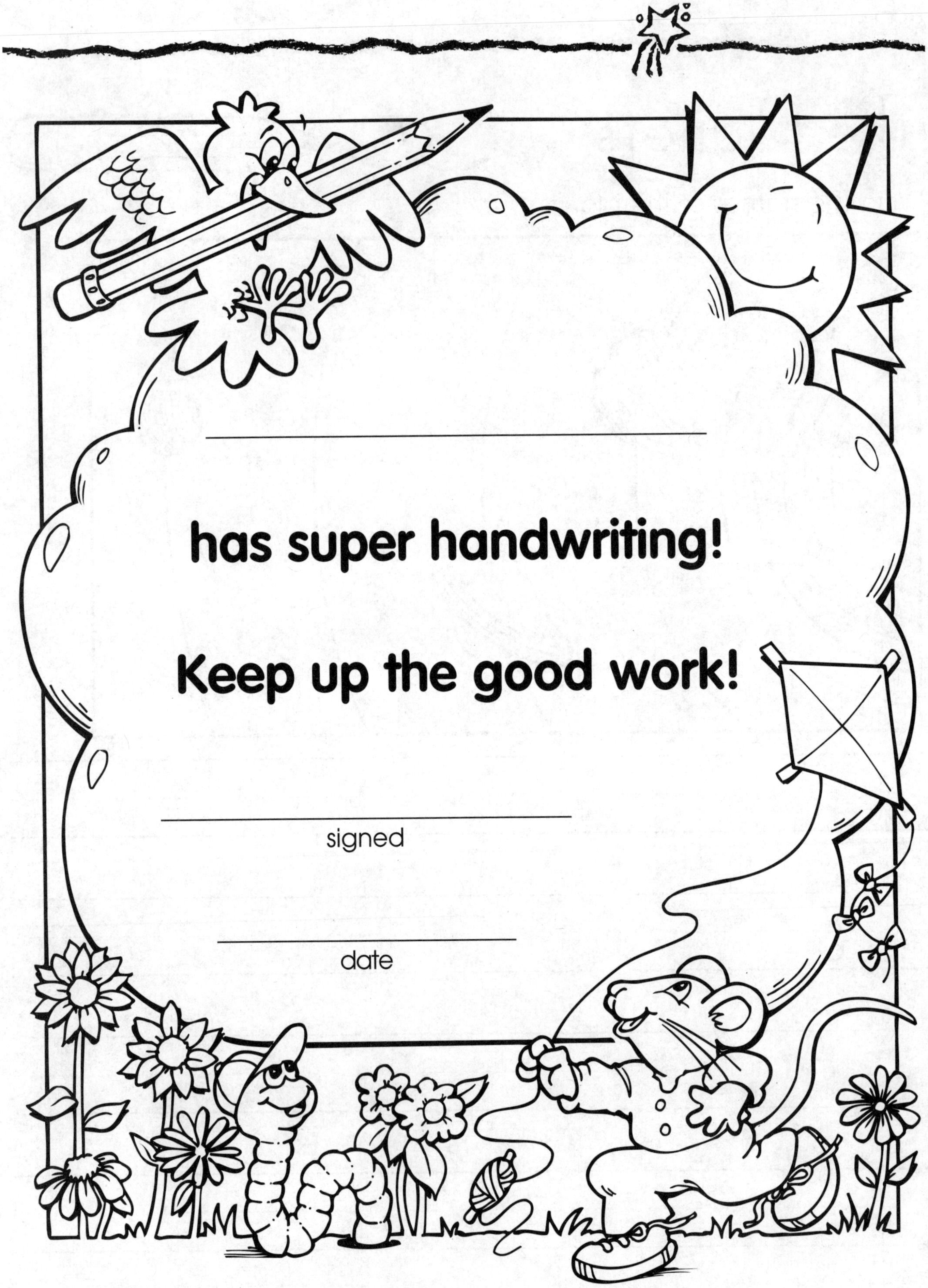

has super handwriting!

Keep up the good work!

signed

date